D0820088

j391.6   Powell, Jillian.
P
              Body decoration.

$16.95

Traditions Around The World
Body Decoration

by Jillian Powell

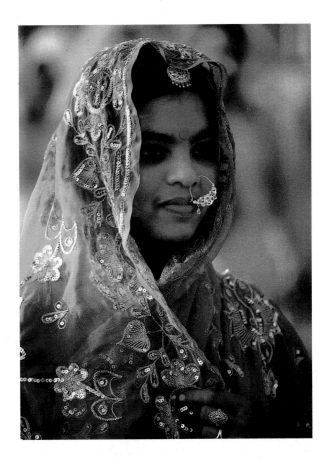

Thomson Learning
New York

Traditions Around The World

Body Decoration

Costumes

Dance

Games

Jewelry

Masks

Consultant: Anthony Shelton, Keeper of Non-Western Art and Anthropology, Royal Pavilion Art Gallery and Museums, Brighton.

First published in the United States in 1995 by Thomson Learning
115 Fifth Avenue
New York, NY 10003

First published in Great Britain in 1994 by Wayland (Publishers) Ltd.

Library of Congress Cataloging-in-Publication Data
Powell, Jillian.
  Body Decoration / Jillian Powell
    p. cm.—(Traditions around the world)
  Includes bibliographical references and index.
  ISBN 1-56847-276-5
  1. Body marking—Juvenile literature. 2. Hairdressing—Juvenile literature. 3. Cosmetics—Juvenile literature.
[1. Body marking. 2. Hairdressing. 3. Cosmetics.]
I. Title. II. Series.
GT2343.P68   1995
391'.6—dc20   94-32624

Printed in Italy

COVER: An Aboriginal man with traditional face decorations, Australia.

Picture acknowledgments:

The publishers wish to thank the following for providing the photographs for this book: Sue Cunningham 19, 23; Ebenezer Pictures 42 (bottom, S. Burton); Eye Ubiquitous 8 (P.M. Field), 16 (Jason Burke), 24-5 (John Miles), 32 (David Cumming); Robert Harding Picture Library 11, 14 (Rob Whitrow), 18-19, 35 (F. Jackson), 36-7 (F. Jackson), 43 (Ian Griffiths), 45; Jim Holmes 6, 33 (top); Skjold 12; South American Pictures 27 (Bill Leimbach); Still Pictures 13 (Mark Edwards), 22-3 (Herbert Girardet); Tony Stone Worldwide *title page*, 26 (Gerard Pile), 28 (Jean-Marie Truchet), 29 (Ben Edwards), 34 (Paul Kenward), 40-41 (Paul Chesley); Tropix Photographic Library 42 (top, D. Charlwood), 44 (D. Charlwood); Wayland Picture Library 6-7, 9, 10-11, 33 (bottom); Zefa Picture Library 15, 17, 20 (both), 31 (Bob Croxford), 36 (J. Bitsch), 38, 39.

The artwork is by Peter Bull.

Contents

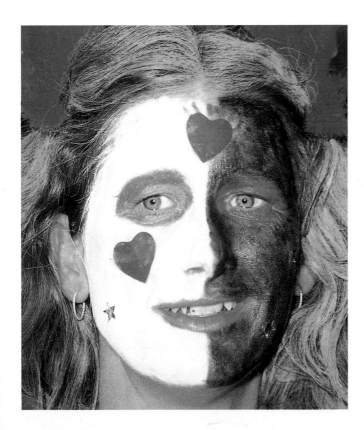

Body decoration around the world

In Europe and ▶
North America
carefully manicured
nails are a sign of
leisure and wealth.

GREENLAND

NORTH
CANADA

AMERICA
U S A

MEXICO

CENTRAL
AMERICA

BRAZIL

PERU

SOUTH

AMERICA

A Kayapo child from South
America. Even very young
children wear some form of
body decoration. ▼

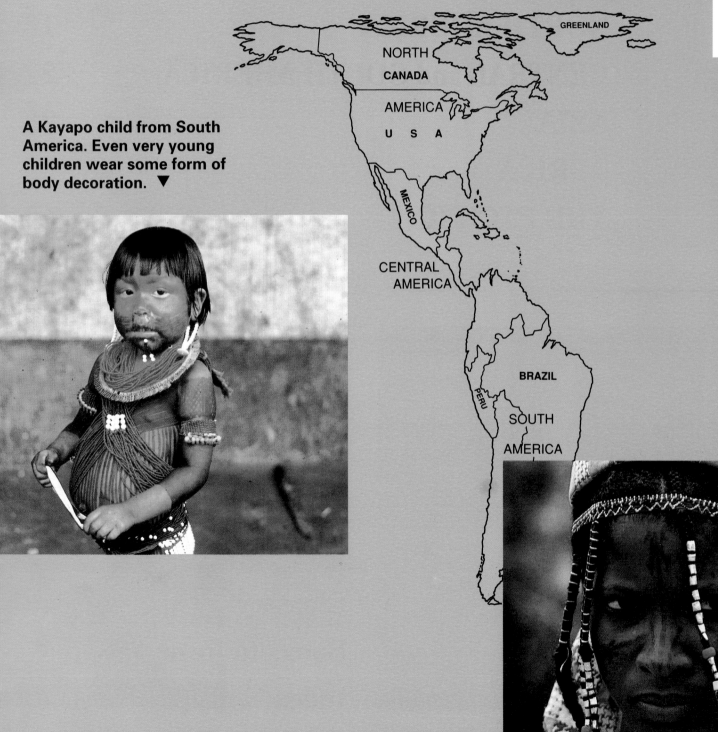

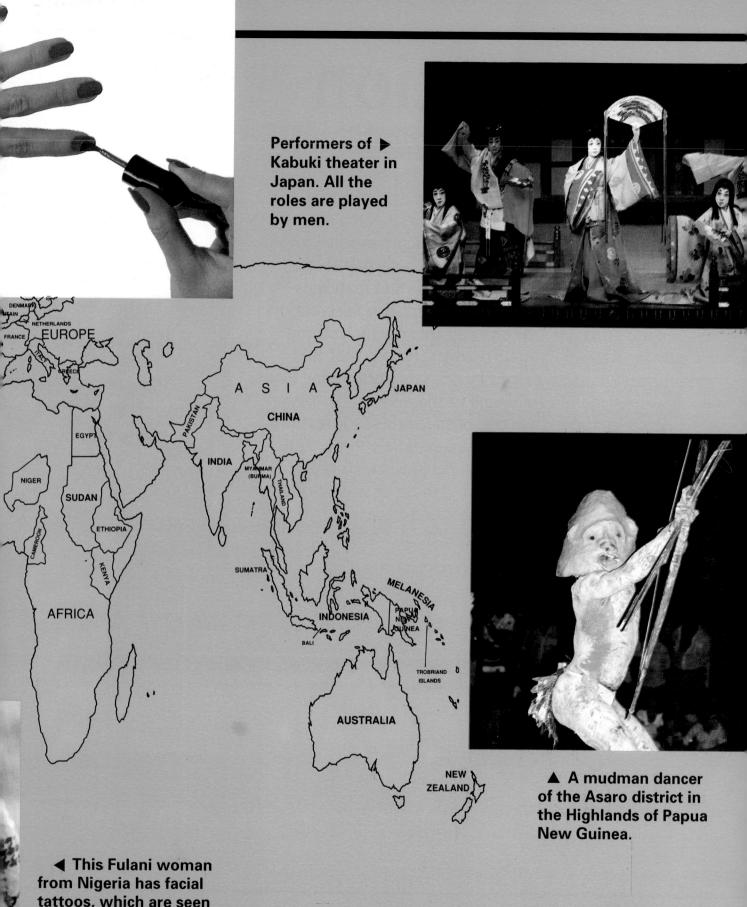

Performers of ▶
Kabuki theater in
Japan. All the
roles are played
by men.

DENMARK
BRITAIN
NETHERLANDS
FRANCE
EUROPE
ITALY
GREECE

ASIA
JAPAN

CHINA
EGYPT
PAKISTAN

NIGER
INDIA
MYANMAR
(BURMA)
SUDAN
THAILAND
ETHIOPIA
CAMEROON
KENYA
SUMATRA
MELANESIA
AFRICA
INDONESIA
PAPUA
NEW
GUINEA
BALI
TROBRIAND
ISLANDS

AUSTRALIA

NEW
ZEALAND

▲ A mudman dancer
of the Asaro district in
the Highlands of Papua
New Guinea.

◀ This Fulani woman
from Nigeria has facial
tattoos, which are seen
as both a sign of beauty
and a form of protection
against evil spirits.

Introduction

Body decoration has been practiced in every culture throughout history. Every part of the body has been decorated, using every kind of method and material. These range from permanent decorations, such as tattoos and scars (sometimes called cicatrization), to temporary ones, such as makeup and body painting. Each culture chooses its own methods and materials and creates its own styles and traditions. Body decoration that appears attractive to one culture may look strange or ugly to another. Fashion changes, too, so that the makeup and hairstyles worn by one generation may look unappealing and old-fashioned to the next.

Body decoration was one of the earliest expressions of art, practiced by men and women of Paleolithic and Neolithic times. In parts of Europe, bowls with red and black pigments and sharp-pointed flints or needles made from bone and antler have been found in caves, suggesting that tattooing was practiced. Little stone

◀ **Long hair may be braided and decorated with coins, beads, and other decorations, as worn here in Xinxiang, China.**

6

figures found in Europe, dating from the Neolithic period, have spiral markings carved on the face and head, and similar marks can be seen on Japanese pottery figures from 2000 B.C. The ancient Egyptians were skilled in the art of makeup and wig making, and the ancient Britons painted their skin and hair blue with a plant dye called woad.

For centuries, face and body paints have been made by grinding colored stone, clays, and plants, then mixing them with vegetable oil or animal fat. The roots of a plant may be used or the leaves boiled, dried and crushed into a powder ready for mixing with oil. The paint is then applied using fingers, hands, or twig or grass brushes, or it is pierced into the skin as tattoo marks using thorns, sharp sticks, or needles. In some parts of the world, these centuries-old methods survive, but in the developed Western world, face and body paints have become part of the cosmetics industry. This industry produces special products including colored creams and powders to shade the eyelids, lipsticks to gloss and color the mouth, mascaras to darken and lengthen eyelashes, and polishes to color nails.

There are many motives for decorating the body. Body decoration can be used to make someone feel and look more attractive to others. Body painting, tattoos, cicatrization, piercing, and hairstyles can show that a person

Face paint and piercing are used for ▶ traditional performance art in Calcutta, India. The man also holds a tongue made of painted wood in his mouth.

belongs to a certain group, clan, or religion. For nomadic peoples, who travel in search of pasture for cattle and who carry few possessions, it may be the chief means of artistic expression. Some peoples decorate their bodies to express closeness to their gods or to the animals with whom they share their environment. Others try to make themselves look different from animals. Body hair may be shaved, for example, and in some cultures the teeth are filed and colored in order to make them look different from animal fangs.

Among hunter-gatherer peoples, and where warfare is practiced, body decoration may be applied for camouflage, but it also may be used to draw attention to the body, for example during special courtship or gift-exchange ceremonies. People may decorate their bodies as part of a celebration or to mark an important event or stage in their lives such as marriage, giving birth, or mourning a loved one. The decoration chosen for skin and hair can also reflect the way a society is organized. Certain decorations are reserved for chiefs and leaders, and others mark differences between sexes and age groups or show marital or other status within a society. In some cultures, only the highest ranks are allowed to wear tattoos. Among the Maori of New Zealand, for example, elaborate facial tattoos were traditionally considered a mark of distinction.

In Melanesia, the number of lines in a facial tattoo once indicated achievements in battle or in the community. In modern Europe and North America, tattooing has become fashionable in the armed services and among various alternative groups of people. Like the piercing of the ears, nose, cheeks, and tongue, tattooing has also become a symbol of rebellion for young people, a sign that they refuse to conform to the kind of body decoration generally accepted by the society in which they live. Wherever it is practiced, body decoration is both a means of self-expression and a form of language or communication to others.

Hair is an important part of body decoration. Hair may be grown long, cut or shaved, dyed, straightened or curled, braided, or elaborately styled. The ancient Egyptians wound hair on wooden sticks, covered it with mud, and baked it into wigs. Beards were worn only by rulers and the upper classes and were styled short or long according to rank. Even women wore artificial ceremonial beards to show their status. In many parts of Africa, hair has been treated like sculpture, built up with clay, animal fat, bones, and beads into such tall, elaborate styles that special headrests had to be used to protect them. Hair can be styled to show age, status, or membership of a tribe. Rendille women, who live in the northern desert of Kenya, wear their hair

sculptured with mud, animal fat, and ocher to show that they have given birth to their first son. When the boy is circumcised to mark his growing up, or when a male relative dies, the woman's head is shaved. Hair also may be shaved to express religious faith, although some religions demand long, uncut hair.

In Western societies, white, even teeth are admired, and people sometimes wear metal braces or have dental surgery to straighten their teeth. The Toposa, a cattle-herding tribe in Africa, extract their lower teeth to force their upper teeth to stick out because they see this as beautiful. Some peoples chip or file their teeth and color them, either for beauty or to protect the teeth or, like the Dogon of Africa, to reflect their myths about the origins of speech.

Body decoration may even extend to altering the shape of the body. Head-shaping, an ancient practice that dates back to pre-Neolithic cultures in Europe and America, still survives in parts of Africa, Greenland, and Peru. Babies' heads are elongated or flattened by binding them with braided leaves or strips of bark, or by using special cradle boards. Some Native American peoples admired a flat skull. The Mangbetu of Africa considered a long head shape beautiful and believed that it also encouraged intelligence and protected against witchcraft. The elongated shape was then emphasized by high hairstyles supported by ivory sticks.

◄ **Rastafarians express their cultural and religious identity through long, uncut hair.**

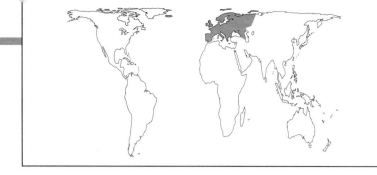

Europe

In Europe, the cosmetics industry has become big business, with vast sums of money spent on advertising new products every year. In the last thirty years, there have been great improvements in the quality and appearance of products specially created to decorate eyes, lips, the rest of the face, and nails. Modern makeup is designed to make the wearer look and feel healthier, younger, and more attractive. It is mainly worn by women, although some makeup and skin-care products are now being used by men. Compared with body decoration in other parts of the world, modern makeup is generally only used to make people's faces look more attractive. Eyeshadows, applied as creams, powders, or pencils, draw attention to the color and shape of the eyes. Eyeliners and mascaras color or darken the lashes and make the eyes look larger. Lipsticks and lip pencils outline, color, and gloss the lips. Blushers and highlighters draw attention to the cheekbones and help emphasize the shape and contours of the face. Foundations and powders even out skin tones, giving a smooth, healthy-looking complexion and hiding shadows, blemishes, and even scars. Body makeup may be used to give a healthy glow to the skin, and fingernails and toenails may be painted and glossed with colored polishes.

In this medieval painting, you can see the high ▶ foreheads that were fashionable during the Middle Ages.

▲ **In the 1960s, many women wore pale makeup and hair extensions.**

Over the centuries, body decoration has changed with fashion. In the Middle Ages, the eyebrows were plucked away and the hairline was shaved to give extra height to the forehead. Later, in the eighteenth century, black patches or beauty spots were worn on the face to emphasize the whiteness of the skin. Tastes change and today, despite warnings of the risks of skin cancer from too much sun, many people enjoy lying in the sun to develop deep even tans in order to convey a sense of good health.

Dark red lipstick was popular in the 1940s, and eyebrows were plucked into fine lines emphasized with dark eye pencils. By the 1960s, however, pale pastel-colored lipsticks had become popular and all the attention was drawn to the eyes by eyeshadows, eyeliners, mascaras, and even false eyelashes. Today there is more variety in the styles of makeup worn, from a natural look to fantasy styles and bright colors.

11

Special makeup is worn by stage and television actors to change or emphasize their features. ▶

People in European countries sometimes use face painting to celebrate holidays, carnivals, or special events. In Sweden, children paint their faces to look like witches at Easter. In Great Britain (as in the U.S.), there is a similar custom for children to make themselves up to look like witches, ghosts, or skeletons on Halloween. In the Netherlands and Italy, people paint their faces in bright colors at carnival time. Soccer supporters sometimes paint their faces in the colors of their team for an important game, and in Ireland some people paint shamrocks on their cheeks and dye their hair green to celebrate St. Patrick's Day. In many cities, face painting and hair braiding and beading are now popular street activities, at fairs and any number of celebrations. You can have your face painted to look like an animal, a bird, or in any design you like! For face painting, special crayons and paints that will not harm the skin or irritate the eyes are used.

Special face paint is worn by actors and actresses in the theater. Theatrical makeup enables a character's features to show up under bright stage lighting. It can often be used to alter facial structure and appearance. Putty or wax may be used to change the shape of the nose, chin, or forehead. Modern theatrical makeup used in productions such as *Cats* and *Phantom of the Opera* is an art in its own right.

The traditional European clown's makeup is believed to have originated in France in the seventeenth century. Two comic actors who had once been bakers are said to have created the first greasepaint makeup by greasing their faces with animal fat and dusting them with white flour. Greasepaint makeup was made from about 1860, using animal fats and chalk. Clowns in different parts of the world have different ways of making up their faces, but the most famous is "whiteface" with red and black markings, which was first worn by the sad clown Pierrot in France. Every clown creates his or her own design and has unique makeup. The mouth is usually exaggerated, turning upward or downward, and tears may be painted falling from the eyes. Clowns often have bright red noses and cheeks and very pointed or shaggy eyebrows.

Bright face paints and dyed hair worn for the Copenhagen Carnival in Denmark ▶

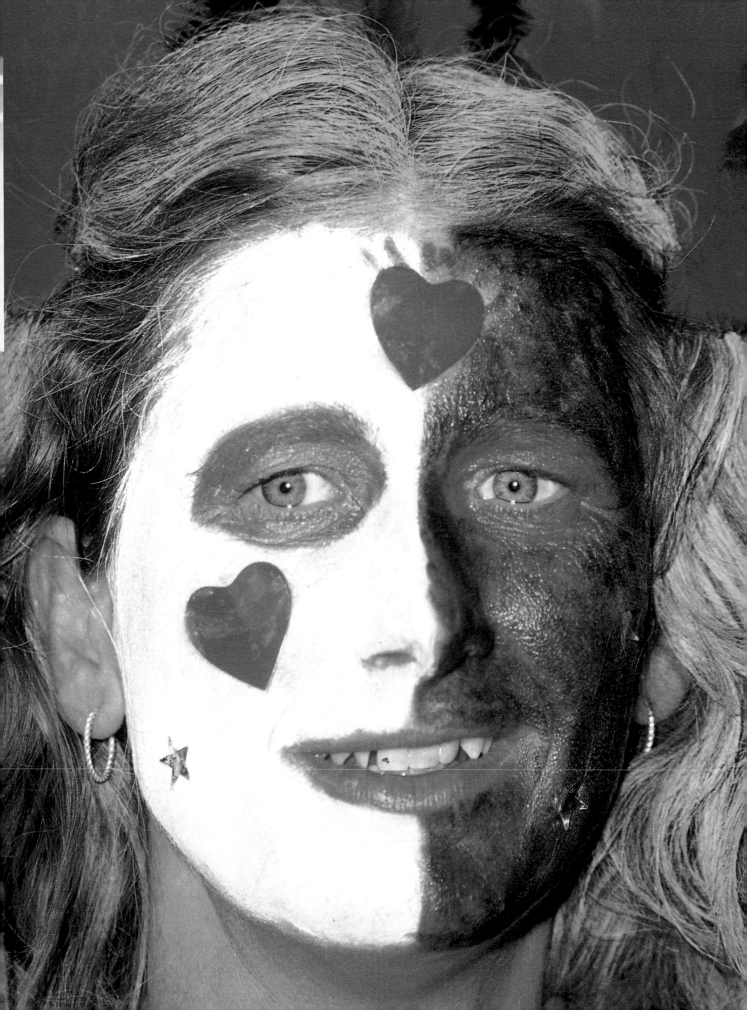

Tattooing has been practiced in Europe since ancient times. For the ancient Greeks, it was a sign of nobility, but it has also been used to brand prisoners and slaves. Although tattooing had been known in Europe for centuries, it had been outlawed until Captain Cook's voyage to the South Sea Islands in 1769 that led to a revival. The word *tattoo* comes from the Tahitian word *tatau*. The Tahitians pierced the skin using sharp combs of bone or shell dipped in an ink which they made from the soot produced by burning oily groundnuts. Sailors spread the practice to Europe, and today it still remains popular among sailors, as well as with those who use tattooing to denote belonging to a group or as a means of individual expression.

Modern electric needles have made the process of tattooing quicker and less painful, enabling some people to have large areas of the body tattooed, although the chest and arms remain the most common parts for this kind of body decoration. Popular motifs include the names of loved ones, often with hearts or flowers. Members of alternative groups such as punks often choose words or symbols of rebellion, such as the skull and crossbones or antipolice slogans. They also may wear facial tattoos designed to shock, such as a spider on its web. Tattooing is permanent and can be difficult and expensive to remove, but now there are colored paper transfers available that imitate tattoos but can be worn just until they are washed away.

**Some tattoo enthusiasts have much of ▶
their bodies covered with colorful designs.**

Piercing, for wearing studs or other decorations, has recently become popular among young people in European cities. Although ear piercing has long been common among females, it is now fashionable with both sexes. The earlobe and rim may be pierced several times. The nose, cheeks, and even tongue may be pierced with studs, chains, or safety pins.

The punk movement began on the streets of London, England, in the late 1970s. As well as having facial and body tattoos and piercing their faces and tongues, punks dyed their hair bright colors. They often wore it partly shaved and spiked into spectacular shapes, such as the Mohawk, inspired by a Native American people.

**The punk look, ▶
complete with dyed
Mohawk and facial
makeup.**

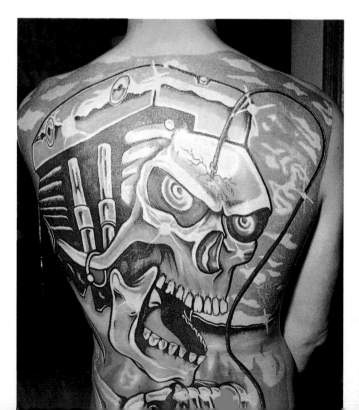

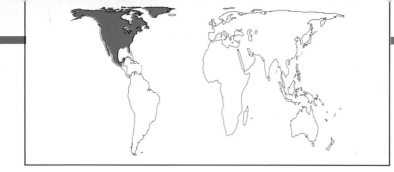

North America

Though North Americans use body decoration – most notably facial makeup – to look more attractive just as the Europeans do, there is a definite emphasis on conveying a youthful and healthy appearance. Foundation, powders, and blushers help the skin look younger and healthier. Eye shadows and mascaras help brighten the eyes. Lips look fuller and more alluring when lipstick is worn. In Western cultures body decoration is used to disguise the effects of age. Gray or white hair may be colored with dyes. Thinning hair and baldness may be disguised by wigs or hair transplants. Cosmetic surgery may be used, such as injecting collagen to plump out the skin or lips.

Dentistry is used to straighten teeth with metal braces or to cap uneven or chipped teeth. Gold or silver caps with designs in them are sometimes worn, even if the tooth underneath is healthy. Teeth also may be whitened cosmetically with polishes. For many women, it is important to decorate nails. Carefully manicured nails are a sign of leisure and wealth, just as in Imperial China, where one nail was grown very long to show that no manual work was done. Nails are filed into shape and painted with colored polishes that range from transparent and natural pinks to vivid reds, purples, and black. Fake nails, which were popular in

Shaving part of the head to form decorative patterns is a popular style of body decoration. ▼

16

the 1960s, have been replaced by wraps or extensions, which give the appearance of long, strong nails. Toenails are generally worn shorter, but may also be polished.

The earlobes of females, and increasingly of males, may be pierced for wearing earrings. Piercing has become very popular among the young, who may have their ears, noses, cheeks, tongues, and other parts of their bodies pierced for wearing studs, rings, chains, or other decorations. As in Europe, tattooing of the face and body has also become fashionable among young people, who often compete with one another for the wildest and most adventurous designs.

◀ **In the West, nails may be polished to fit a person's mood or to match clothing.**

Styling the hair is an important part of body decoration in North America. Hairstyles change with fashion, so that while it was usual for men to wear long hair or wigs in earlier centuries, in the first half of the twentieth century men's hair was generally worn short. It was not until the 1960s, with the influence of the British rock group the Beatles and hippie culture, that longer styles began to be worn again. Women's hair has been styled in many different ways, using various methods, from heated curlers and tongs to tying up sections with strips of rags.

Today, both men and women wear their hair long or short, shaved or partly shaved. Hair may be cut in traditional styles, such as a one-length bob for

▲ **Elaborate braiding and beading, long popular among many peoples around the world, has enjoyed a revival in the West.**

18

women or "crew-cut" for men, or it may be geometrically cut in a wedge or any unusual shape.

Hair colorants, which may be permanent, semipermanent, or wash-out dyes, are widely available in hair salons and for home use. Modern colorants are easy and clean to use and offer a wide range of natural or artificial colors. Natural-looking shades may improve the hair's own color. Colors also can be used to highlight sections of hair, perhaps adding fun colors such as royal blue or purple-red. These kinds of colors are popular among youth groups. The texture of the hair also may be changed. Naturally curly hair can be straightened. Straight hair can be permed or waved or simply given the appearance of more volume and thickness by the use of perming lotions.

The Huichol of northwest Mexico hold festivals to celebrate the planting and harvesting of their most important crop, corn. They prepare by painting their faces with bright, corn-colored patterns. They grind the root of the uxa plant, a kind of small bush, into a yellow paste and draw patterns on their faces with pieces of straw. Like the textiles they weave, the designs are often symbolic, with parallel lines representing the boundaries of the cornfields, and rows of dots representing the growing corn.

◀ **Tarahumara men from Mexico, decorated with body paint for a traditional dance and ceremony**

◀ Nowadays, Native Americans decorate their bodies for traditional ceremonies, often watched by tourists.

Many Native Americans traditionally wear their hair long, sometimes braided or beaded. This Navajo man is wearing hair wraps. ▼

Native Americans of the United States and Canada were skilled face painters. They painted their faces for camouflage when hunting, to appear fierce and brave in battle, for sports competitions, and when mourning dead loved ones. Face paints also protected their skin against the sun and wind. They made paint by grinding rocks, clays, or plants in mortars or rubbing them on flat stones. They mixed the colored powders with water or animal fat and applied them with their hands or with a reed that they had chewed or pounded to make a brush. They sometimes put paint in their mouths and sprayed each other with color. For dances and ceremonies, ritual designs and colors (including symbols of their ancestors and clans) were carefully applied on the foreheads and cheeks. Face painting was just one part of the elaborate decorations worn by Native Americans. Both men and women painted their faces and had their ears and noses pierced for decoration. Some groups, such as the Mohave, also wore tattoos on their chins.

20

Paint your face like the Iroquois

To paint your face like the Iroquois, you will need water-based makeup or greasepaint and some tissues or paper towels. For water-based makeup, you will need some jars of water and two or three watercolor brushes. For greasepaint you will need to prepare your skin with a layer of cold cream.

1. Divide your face into two sections by drawing a black line from ear to ear, about halfway up your nose.

2. Paint the bottom half of your face reddish-brown and paint the top half yellow.

3. Draw a semicircular line in black on either side of your face, making a circle with the shape of your ear.

4. Add some spokes, radiating inward from the semicircle.

Different groups had different ways of painting their faces. Some used geometric designs, with zigzag lines on the forehead and spots on the cheeks. The Haida painted motifs such as the sun or hawks' tails over the mouth or the brow. They used bold colors like red and black.

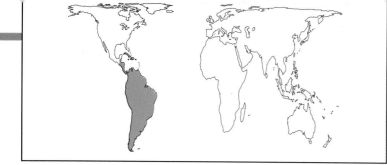

Central and South America

Body painting is widely practiced among the Native Americans of Central and South America. In Brazil, there are many groups, each with its own culture and language, living in the Xingu Park. These peoples are hunter-gatherers, skilled at fishing and in the arts of pottery and textile weaving. It is generally the younger people who paint their bodies. They bathe in the rivers, shave off their body hair, and make their skin glisten with a thick red paste made from a plant called urucu or anatto. They split the red seeds open by rubbing them on woven straw mats, then boil them in clay pots kept outside the huts. The urucu paste is molded into balls and stored in banana leaves. Both men and women paint their bodies with urucu mixed with the oil of the *pequí* fruit, although the women wear a paler color than the men. Urucu paste is also rubbed into the hair, which is often cut in a circular shape and decorated with geometric patterns in charcoal. Even babies are painted with the red paste.

South American ▶ Indians such as the Kayapo decorate even babies and small children with body and face paint and ear and lip piercing.

Strong, geometric designs ▶
are used for body painting,
such as this Megrianoti
design from the Xingu
Park, Brazil.

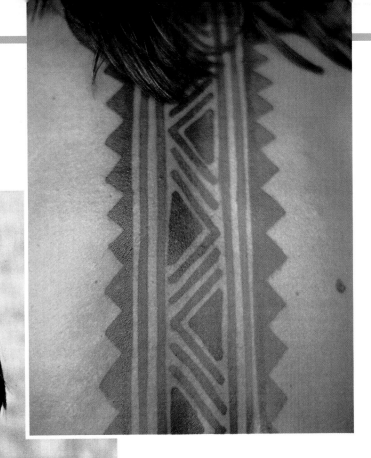

Txicâo men paint themselves with urucu in bold, rectangular designs set against black charcoal, with fringes of down from the egret. The Txucarramâe paint their bodies with charcoal and the blue-black juice of the genipip fruit. The patterns of their body decoration are among the most complex to be found among the Brazilian Indians, and range from delicate filigree designs, which look like clinging lace garments, to bold, abstract shapes. Both men and women grow their hair long over their shoulders but shave their heads above the forehead. A bald or shaven head may relate to moon myths and worship. For the peoples of the Xingu, color has symbolic power. Red symbolizes blood and therefore life; yellow, the sun, which is an important part of their mythology and religion; and black, the night.

Indigenous South American peoples decorate themselves for ceremonies, important events, and visits. When the Karaya of eastern Brazil visit neighboring villages, they prepare for the journey by painting themselves with urucu paste. The host villagers also paint their faces with urucu and charcoal as a sign of welcome. Special decoration is worn by Brazilian peoples for the Javari, a semireligious festival held in summer, when ceremonial games are played with spears blunted with beeswax. The men taking part paint their bodies with spotted designs imitating the leopard-cat of their mythology.

The Mekrangnontíre hold a special women's ceremony. Young girls prepare themselves by painting their faces and bodies with urucu and decorating them with fringes of egret down and with crushed blue eggshell around the forehead. Another ceremony in which women take part is the Yamuricamá. This celebrates a legend in which the men of the village disappeared and the women, having searched for a long time, lost hope and adopted the ways of men: fishing, hunting, and wearing men's headdresses, earrings, and other decorations. During the ceremony, which begins early in the morning, the women sing, dance, and decorate themselves like men. Their bodies are painted with designs in red and black. Black markings on their faces, made with a kind of resin, show their relationship to the chief's family group.

Young Arara girls from the Xingu Park, ▶ decorated with jaguar designs

◄ Both men and women may have the nose and other parts of the face pierced for decoration, like this Mejecodoteri woman from Venezuela.

Many indigenous peoples practice piercing and decoration of the ears and lips to show membership of a family or group, to mark an important stage or event in life, or to reflect their beliefs and mythology. Piercing is usually carried out using sharp bones or thorns, with plant leaves, feathers, and colored wood used for decoration. Tchikrin boys and girls are decorated when they are babies. A boy has his earlobes pierced by his father at birth, and red wooden ear disks are worn. His lower lip is pierced with a string of beads. His eyebrows and forehead are shaved and his mother, grandmother, and other relatives paint linear designs on his body. At the age of eight, when he leaves his mother to live in the men's huts at the center of the village, his hair is cut and his body is painted black. When he is older he will have his hair cut like the adults and wear the larger lip disk of the men.

Txucarramâe boys wear lip disks made of a lightweight wood called sara. As they grow older, the disks are replaced with larger ones, up to 4 inches in diameter. Plants are also used for ear decorations, such as the leaves of the inajá palm. These are tightly rolled, then stiffened and painted with a chalk-white powder taken from river clay. The most highly prized decorations are feathers like those of the toucan and other colorful forest birds. These are attached with cotton threads and beeswax to a sharpened straw that pierces the ear. For ceremonies, special lip and ear disks, decorated with tassels or beads, are worn.

These decorations may carry symbolic meaning. The Suya of Brazil pierce children's ears to show that they must listen to their elders. The ear disk is believed to help learning and show wisdom. The lips are pierced to show that a child is gaining in speech and understanding. For adult males, lip piercing represents skills in speaking and also in warfare. Color, too, may be symbolic, with red associated with bravery and warfare and white representing wisdom and understanding.

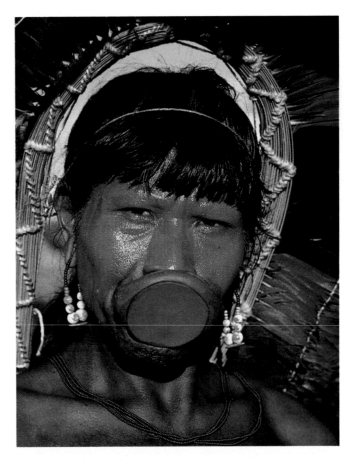

▲ A Kayapo chief, decorated with urucum and a lip plate. The larger the plate, the more impressive the decoration.

Asia

▲ The red mark on this Indian woman's forehead shows that she is married. Her nose decoration is also a sign of marriage and wealth.

In India and Pakistan, it is a tradition for women to decorate their hands and feet with henna for happy occasions, especially weddings. This is practiced by women of the Hindu, Muslim, and Sikh faiths and is a social rather than a religious custom. A special party is held at the bride's house before a wedding. Friends paint delicate, lacelike patterns on her palms and the soles of her feet using an orange henna paste called mehndi. At Hindu weddings, it is customary for the groom to paint the bride's hair parting red as a sign that she is married.

The forehead is an important focus for body decoration in India. Hindus believe that the "third eye," the eye of wisdom, is located between the eyebrows. This eye can be "opened" by meditation and devotion. During religious ceremonies, a tilak, or mark of ground sandalwood and saffron paste, is worn on the forehead by men and women as a sign of a pure, holy life. Women wear a bindi, or a mark of red paste made from kumkum powder, on the forehead to show they are married. Young women may also paint or stick on colored marks for decoration. When dressing up for special occasions, small dots of color may be painted over the eyebrows. At one time, facial tattoos were worn, as it was believed that they were a protection against evil spirits.

A woman paints delicate patterns of henna paste, or mehndi, onto a customer's palm and fingers in Kolhapur, India. ▶

Decorate your hands with mehndi

Henna is used to decorate the hands and feet in India, parts of Africa, and the Middle East.

You will need some powdered henna; the juice of a lemon; a little cold, brewed tea; and a long, blunt hairpin.

1. Mix the henna powder, lemon juice, and cold tea into a paste.

2. Open the hairpin and use one end to dip into the paste and paint fine patterns. You could try a crisscross pattern with dots between the lines, or small ovals covering the palm. You could also include your initials in the tradition of Indian brides, who wear their husbands' initials.

3. Let your hands dry for about half an hour.

4. You can fix the pattern by dabbing on a solution of lemon juice and sugar. The mehndi should last about three weeks.

▲ **Dramatic face paint worn at the Chinese opera school in Taiwan.**

In southwest India, actors and actresses paint their faces with fantastic, colorful designs for the Kathakali theater. The audience can recognize gods, demons, and other characters from myths and legends in the plays by the colors and patterns painted on their faces. The performers lie on the floor while their faces are painted using pieces of bamboo dipped in colored powders mixed with coconut oil. It can take four hours to paint a Kathakali face.

In China, a special kind of face painting called lien p'u is worn by singers performing opera. Chinese opera dates back thousands of years and may have been influenced by ancient Indian theater. Many different stories with characters such as gods, heroes, villains, and comics are performed. All the characters are played by men. Each type of character has its own style of makeup, which is said to reflect its true nature: lien p'u means "the face that shows a record."

For more than a thousand years, the Chinese practiced foot binding. A girl's feet were usually bound when she was about six or seven years old. As she grew, the bandages were tightened so that the foot remained small, except for the big toe, which was needed for balance. The "Lotus foot" was a sign of noble birth and was considered beautiful and dainty.

Many Indian women have their ears and noses pierced for jewelry. Noses may be decorated with studs, rings, or jeweled decorations that are linked by a fine chain to earrings or woven into the hair. These are signs of marriage and wealth.

◄ Padaung "giraffe women" from Myanmar (formerly Burma). Their huge rattan and brass collars indicate their rank in society.

In Myanmar (formerly Burma), the Padaung women of the Kayah state have been called "giraffe women" because of their elongated necks. The Padaung are one of the hill peoples living close to the Thai border. The women stretch their necks by wearing collars of rattan enclosed in beaten brass. As they age, the number of rings is gradually increased, forcing down their ribs and collar bones and elongating the neck. This stretches the neck muscles, leaving them incapable of supporting the head's weight without the rings. These collars are symbols of the women's status in society, although today they are usually seen only on older women because the practice is declining among the young. At one time, if a woman was unfaithful to her husband, she was punished by having her neck rings removed, which meant that her head had to be held up or supported all the time.

In parts of Indonesia, tooth filing is practiced to mark the progression from childhood to adulthood or as a sign that a woman is of noble birth. Women's teeth are chipped or filed in Sumatra and Bali during special tooth-filing ceremonies.

In Japan, the art of tattooing, Irezumi, has a long history. Glazed clay tomb figures dating from ancient times show facial tattoos that may have had religious or magical meanings as well as being signs of beauty. In the seventeenth and eighteenth centuries, tattooing was very popular, and artists like Utamaro did designs for tattoos. Later, tattooing became associated with gangsters and geisha girls, and in the nineteenth century it was banned by the emperor. However, tattooing has been revived during the twentieth century.

Japanese tattoo artists once used bamboo sticks with 30 needles attached that pierced the skin up to 120 times per minute. Traditionally, Irezumi covers the body with colorful designs including peony and cherry blossoms, pine trees, landscapes, dragons, birds, tigers, and other animals. Many of the images are symbolic: dragons represent wisdom, carp represents bravery, and peonies stand for wealth and good fortune.

▲ In Nepal, as in other parts of Asia, the ankles and soles of the feet may be decorated as well as the hands.

Irezumi is worn and applied mainly by men. Working from his own sketches, the tattoo artist draws the design onto the skin with a felt pen. He tattoos one section at a time, outlining it with a charcoal-based ink before filling in the colors. The deeper the needle goes, the stronger the color. Masters of the art can achieve delicate shading by inserting needles to different depths. Irezumi that covers the body may take 100 hours of work.

A special kind of makeup is worn for the Japanese Kabuki theater, which dates back to the sixteenth century. Kumadori makeup is worn by actors playing gods, heroes, villains, or demons. Men also play women or young boys and wear plainer, mainly white, makeup. Kumadori means "pattern taking." The lines painted on the face are said to follow the course of the blood in the character's veins according to his or her mood – peaceful or angry, happy or sad. The actor applies his own makeup, using his fingers or fine brushes.

◄ Male actors playing women in the Kabuki theater of Japan.

33

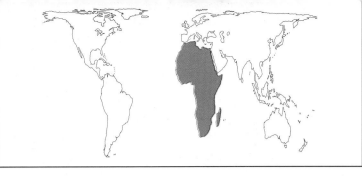

Africa

There is a rich tradition of body painting among the peoples of Africa. Painting the face and body is part of everyday social life, as well as a preparation for important events or rituals. The Bangwa of Cameroon oil their skin and hair daily with powdered leaves, bark, and wood. When they are celebrating a marriage or birth or crowning a new chief, they rub their bodies with red-gold camwood powder, because for them red symbolizes life and joy. For funerals, mourners smear their bodies with dark clays. Sometimes the patterns show their relationship to the dead person.

The southeast Nuba people of the Kordofan province of Sudan paint their bodies to celebrate youth, beauty, and strength. Even newborn children are decorated with red and yellow ochers. Young people bathe, shave, and oil their bodies with sesame, cottonseed, or peanut oil before dusting themselves with colored powders such as yellow ocher and white limestone. Designs are drawn on with the fingers or brushes of grass or straw. Some are abstract; others imitate animals or insects, such as leopards, giraffes, or wasps.

Special body decoration is worn for fights or courtship ceremonies. The Surma, a seminomadic people of Ethiopia, prepare for stick fights by covering their skin with chalk and water, sometimes mixed with yellow ocher, and drawing patterns with their fingers. Top fighters from each village compete, using six-foot-long sticks. The body paint is designed to impress their opponents and the women who watch.

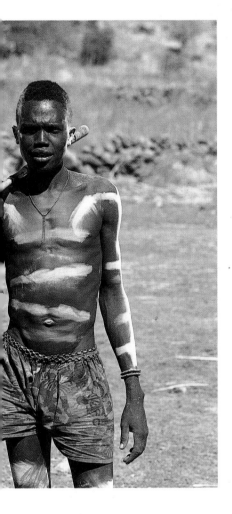

▲ Ash and mud, as worn by this Nuba man from Sudan, are sometimes used to show mourning for a dead loved one.

◀ Many African peoples, like the Kikuyu of Kenya, paint their faces and bodies for traditional ceremonies.

35

Young Fulani men of Niger spend hours decorating for the annual Geerewol Festival. They paint their faces with yellow ocher, using black kohl to show up the whiteness of their teeth and eyes. A white line is painted along the nose and the forehead is shaved to enhance the long nose and high forehead that they admire. During the Yaake courtship dance, the men show their teeth and roll their eyes to attract a bride.

Women also decorate themselves for special events. Berber women of the Sahara paint their faces for the Imilchil Fair where sheep, goats, and camels are bought and sold and marriage partners are found. Even small girls paint their faces brightly, with rouge on their eyebrows and spots of kohl on their cheeks, chins, and noses.

Cicatrization, or marking the skin with raised scars, is considered beautiful by many peoples and may be used to mark stages or events in life. The skin is hooked with a thorn, then cut and rubbed with ash to raise the keloids, or thick scars. Among the southeast Nuba, both men and women practice cicatrization. A girl's body is decorated at puberty, when she is pregnant, and when she becomes a mother. Boys are decorated at puberty and on reaching manhood, when scars are seen as a proof of courage. For some tribes, like the Bangwa of Cameroon, scars are a mark of status.

Many peoples use piercing to mark stages in life. A Samburu woman wears a double strand of beads looped from her ears for each son who passes into warriorhood. Elders of the Turkana and Pokot tribes wear aluminum leaf pendants in their noses to announce a daughter's engagement.

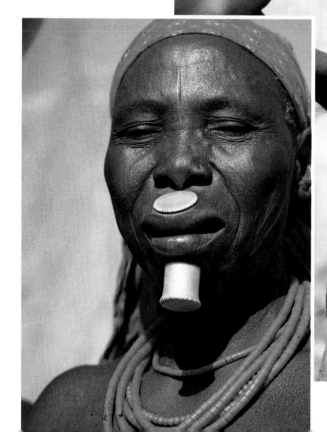

Lip plugs are a sign of beauty and ▶ wealth for some peoples in Africa.

◄ **This young woman of the southeast Nuba has raised keloids, or scars, which are a mark of beauty.**

Lips, noses, and ears are pierced during childhood for wearing decorations. They also show tribal identity and are thought to protect against the supernatural. For the Surma people, a woman's beauty and wealth are measured by the lip plates she wears. The lower lip is pierced in childhood then gradually stretched by inserting larger wooden or clay lip plates. Women may remove the plates when talking together, but not when their husbands are present. The size of the plate determines the number of cattle asked by a bride's parents for her hand in marriage. It is said that originally lip plates were worn to discourage slave traders, or that they related to the worship of broad-beaked birds such as spoonbills. Today, however, the practice is declining among young women.

Ears may be pierced several times around the rim and the lobe extended with an ear disk. When they are small, southeast Nuba girls have their noses, ears, and lips pierced by their mothers or sisters. Beads are worn around the ears and a red bead or ivory rod is worn from a wire through the lower lip. Masai women must always wear earrings to show they are married. Pierced ears, lips, or noses also may relate to tribal myths about the origins of skills such as weaving.

In Africa, many hours may be spent grooming and dressing the hair. For some peoples, hairstyles mark different age groups. Special styles may be worn for rituals or ceremonies or to celebrate major events in life, such as marriage or the birth of a child. Both men's and women's hair may be partly shaved, elaborately braided, or sculpted with sisal, clay, tree bark, or cloth pads. Palm oil, butter, and animal fats are used for dressing the hair. The most complicated styles may take anywhere from several hours to whole days to complete.

Turkana men use clay to sculpt their hair. They twist the hair into small braids, cover these braids with clay, and shape them in buns on top of the head. Ostrich feathers may be woven into the hair as a sign of status. Rendille women of the northern desert of Kenya wear their hair in a crest shape caked with mud, animal fat, and ocher to show that they have given birth to their first son. Wealthy Senegalese women lengthen their hair using sisal fibers and dress it with butter and crushed charcoal. The Hamar of southern Ethiopia construct elaborate hairstyles called *boro* to celebrate a successful hunt or the planting of crops. The hair is trimmed and covered with clay, and colored powders are flicked on with a brush.

For the southeast Nuba, hair can show age and status. A young boy wears his hair shaved into a skullcap and decorated with red or white powders. As he gets older, his hair is allowed to grow and he may use more colors. As an adult he wears his hair in two strips along his head, dressed with beeswax and decorated with charcoal and yellow ocher. Southeast Nuba women dress their hair with oil, ocher, and decorations such as beads and feathers. A girl shaves her head when she is married and again when she becomes a mother.

Two traditional techniques from West Africa that are widely used for African hair are cornrowing, a way of braiding the hair tightly against the scalp to form patterns, and threading, which involves wrapping sections of hair with thick thread to create three-dimensional designs of raised strands.

How to thread your hair

You will need a comb, some hair oil, scissors, and thread the same color as your hair. To create the style called *Onigi* (sticks):

1. Comb your hair out straight and divide it into about 16 equal, square sections. Secure all sections separately, except one, with clips or hair bands. Twist the loose section with oil.

2. Twist three feet of doubled thread around the section of oiled hair, beginning at the scalp and winding it clockwise around the hair until you get to the hair ends.

3. Knot the thread two or three times at the tip of the hair and cut off the end of the thread.

4. Repeat steps 1 – 3 on one section at a time until the hair is completely threaded.

A woman in central Africa ▶
with threaded hair

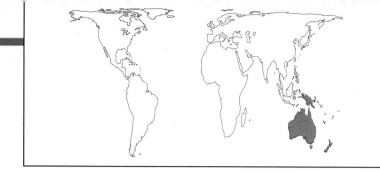

The Pacific

The Aborigines are the native peoples of Australia. When European settlers arrived, their land was taken from them. Today, many Aborigines are struggling to regain their land and to maintain their age-old traditions, such as that of body painting. Members of a family may spend hours painting one another, using red and yellow ochers, white pipe clay, and charcoal applied with fingers or brushes. The patterns they paint are passed down through families or clans and contain symbols representing ancestral history and myths. They are painted on the body for ceremonies like the Intichuma fertility ritual. Male dancers bathe, then paint their bodies with red ocher and clay, with birds' down stuck on with blood. Once painted with his clan's sacred symbols, a man becomes a hero of Dreamtime, or the time of Creation, acting out his own clan's ancestral mythology.

Body decoration is also an important part of becoming an adult. When children are born, their bodies are painted with white clay. Later, the septum of the nose may be pierced, and at puberty aboriginal boys undergo circumcision and cicatrization. The skin is marked with decorative or symbolic patterns, often showing clan membership. At this time, boys are instructed in the history and myths of their clan by their elders.

An aboriginal man in Kimberleys, Australia, ▶ painted for a traditional corroboree, or festival

Aboriginal women paint their bodies to attract men, for ritual and ceremony, and at important stages in life such as reaching puberty and marriage. Designs are painted with fingers or sticks in charcoal, white clay, and red ocher, and may be shared with mothers, sisters, and other relatives.

The Maori people came from tropical islands in the Pacific to settle in New Zealand about 1,000 years ago. They lived in groups with chiefs and were skilled at carving wood, weaving, and elaborate tattooing called Moko. Today, many Maori live in towns and cities. Some are trying to revive ancient Maori traditions and ceremonies. For the Maori, as for all Polynesian peoples, tattooing was a symbol of rank. The chiefs had their faces and bodies tattooed with elaborate spiral designs to make them appear more fierce and

This Maori mother and child are wearing traditional decoration for a reenactment of Maori history in Waitangi, New Zealand. ▼

impressive in battle. The skin was pricked with a sharp chisel or comb of bone or wood, and black pigment was rubbed in. A Maori chief believed that his character was imprinted in his facial tattoos, and he even drew them as his signature on documents and deeds. Maori women also wore tattoos, usually around the mouth and chin or on the forehead and between the eyes, because they believed that this made them look younger and more attractive.

Some of the most spectacular body decoration in the world is found in Papua New Guinea. Both men and women in the Mount Hagen area of the Highlands paint and decorate their bodies for ordinary days, for courtship and gift-exchange ceremonies, and for religious rituals. Body decoration is like a language to these peoples, showing their relationship to their family or clan and to ancestral spirits. To prepare for decoration, they rub their skin with fat and oil to make it shine. Pig fat is stored in bamboo tubes and gourd flasks, and oil is squeezed from red and yellow pandanus fruits. For body and

◀ **Face decoration among the peoples of Papua New Guinea is colorful and dramatic, such as that worn by this Huli man from the Highlands.**

face painting, they use powdered blue, white, and yellow river clays, and the rarer red ocher that comes from brown clay. The clay is wrapped in leaves and baked over a fire, then split open to reveal the red pigment.

There are different styles of face and body painting for men and women, and each style relates to the other body decorations being worn, such as wigs and feather headdresses, as well as to the kind of occasion being celebrated. Designs painted on the face have special names such as the *ndamong mong waep,* or raindrop pattern, or the *waep kerua*, a snakeskin design of interlocking diamonds. For festivals, men paint their faces with black charcoal, using white and touches of red, blue, or yellow to enhance their features. Women and boys paint their faces red and use brighter colors. A man may be identified by his face painting and by the combination of feathers and shells he is wearing, although men from the same clan sometimes use identical designs.

Women wear facial tattoos to show their status in society. A mother may tattoo her daughter with small marks on her forehead, above and below her eyes, and across her cheeks. Her skin is pricked, then rubbed with charcoal and blue dye. Some of the older men have the septum of their noses pierced as well as their ears. Decorations such as shells, pigs' or boars' tusks, feathers, bones, and leaves are chosen for both appearance and symbolic meaning.

Some of the strangest decoration is worn by the mudmen of the Asaro river. Besides smearing their bodies with clay, they completely cover their heads and faces with helmets made from clay baked on a barkcloth frame.

◀ **A mudman of the Asaro district in the Highlands of Papua New Guinea**

The most elaborate body decoration is carried out for Pig Festivals, when pigs are sacrificed to please the ghosts of ancestors, and for ceremonies in which leaders of neighboring groups exchange gifts of pigs or money to settle a marriage or a dispute. Many hours are spent decorating, especially painting the face. Men paint their faces using mirrors or with the help of wives and friends. Traditionally, they paint on charcoal mixed with fat or water, using twigs with soft brushes of leaves, although today modern face paints may also be used. Some areas are left for touches of color, such as red on the nose, and white clay or powder is used to outline the eyes, nose, mouth, and cheeks. Decorations, which may include leaves, shells, bones, pigs' tusks, and scarab beetles, are worn through the pierced nose and ears. Colorful sets of birds' feathers called *køi wal* are chosen for the headdress. Wigs are an important part of body decoration because it is believed that ancestral spirits live in the hair. Men taking part in the exchange ceremonies wear ceremonial wigs made from human hair caked with clay, fringed with animal furs, greased, and brightly painted.

Another important festival is the celebration of the yam harvest on the Trobriand Islands. The yam grows well in the islands' thin soil and represents wealth, life, and strength. The harvest is the highlight of the islanders' year and lasts a month or more. The women carry the yams from each garden to the village for the festival, where some will be awarded the prize for "good gardener."

The peoples of the ▶ Highlands of New Guinea decorate their bodies for important ceremonies such as the Pig Festival, dedicated to ancestral spirits.

▲ For dances and ceremonies, people often help paint one another, like these Bundi men in Papua New Guinea.

They prepare by rubbing their bodies with coconut oil, then decorating them with yellow ocher and flower petals.

Body decoration is also important for singing, dancing, and theater. The Gimi theater, performed by the people who live in the eastern Highlands of Papua New Guinea, takes place at night,

44

by torch, fire, and moonlight. Traveling groups of actors act out scenes from Gimi myths and legends during a drama festival that lasts several nights. Their bodies are streaked with clay and decorated with leaves, representing ancestral spirits. In the flickering light, they look dramatic and mysterious.

In the theater, in ceremonies and rituals, and even in everyday life, body decoration is found in every country. It can establish or change a person's identity, make a statement, or simply make the wearer look more attractive. However it is used, body decoration is an important form of self-expression all over the world.

Glossary

Ancestors The earlier generations of a family.

Britons One of the peoples who lived in Britain before the Anglo-Saxons.

Camouflage To hide or disguise something by matching its color or pattern to that of its surroundings.

Camwood A kind of hard red wood from West Africa.

Cicatrization Decorating the skin with raised marks or scars, called keloids.

Circumcision The act of cutting away the foreskin of the penis.

Clan A family group.

Collagen A substance that may be injected into the lips to make them look fuller.

Concentric circles Circles that share the same center point.

Cook, James (1728 – 79) A British navigator and explorer who claimed the east coast of Australia for Britain.

Cornrowing A method of styling the hair by braiding it tightly against the scalp.

Down Soft, fine birds' feathers.

Filigree A delicate ornamental design.

Gourd A type of fruit similar to a squash.

Greasepaint A kind of makeup mainly used for theater, made with a grease rather than a water base.

Henna A brown dye tinged with red obtained from the henna plant and used as a hair rinse.

Hippie A person whose lifestyle and beliefs reject traditional values and ways of behaving.

Indigenous Coming from a particular region of the world.

Kohl A cosmetic powder that was used originally in Asian and Muslim countries to darken the area around the eyes.

Linear Drawn or painted in straight lines.

Meditation The act of contemplation, or thinking deeply about something, usually spiritual matters.

Middle Ages A period of European history dating from about A.D. 500 to 1500.

Myths/mythology Stories and beliefs about the origins of the world and the forces that made it.

Neolithic Belonging to the New Stone Age, c. 9500 – 1000 B.C.

Nomadic The way of life of a clan or people who travel in order to find water and pasture.

Ocher A name for several types of earth that contain yellow, red, or brown pigments.

Palaeolithic Belonging to the Old Stone Age, c. 35000 – 9500 B.C.

Puberty The age at which a child's body changes, taking on adult sexual characteristics.

Resin A sticky substance extracted from a plant and often used in varnishes and paints. Resin does not dissolve in water.

Ritual A ceremony usually connected with religious or other beliefs.

Shamrock A small, three-leaved plant that is the national emblem of Ireland.

Sisal The natural twine-like fiber.

Status The position of a person within a group or society.

Symbol Something that stands for something else.

Threading A method of styling the hair by wrapping sections in thread.

Woad A plant that produces a blue dye.

Books to read

Caldecott, Barrie. *Jewelry Crafts*. Fresh Start. New York: Franklin Watts, 1992.

Earl, Amanda and Sensier, Danielle. *Masks*. Traditions Around the World. New York: Thomson Learning, 1995.

Jackson, Julia A. *Gemstones: Treaures from the Earth's Crust*. Earth Resources. Hillside, NJ: Enslow Publishers, 1989.

Rosen, Mike. *Summer Festivals*. Seasonal Festivals. New York: Bookwright Press, 1991.

Sensier, Danielle. *Costumes*. Traditions Around the World. New York: Thomson Learning, 1995.

Information about individual cultures may also be found in the 48-volume Cultures of the World series by Marshall Cavendish Corporation (North Bellmore, NY), or in your library's encyclopedia.

Index

The body decorations in this book come from many different peoples. Various types of decoration are listed in the index, such as "tattoos," "piercing," and "face painting." If you want to see how body decoration is used, look at entries such as "ceremonies" and "festivals." You can use the "peoples" entry to look up body decoration from the different cultures mentioned in the book.